FORCE JANE BRETTLE

FORCE

Essays by Louise A. Jackson and Amanda Hopkinson
National Galleries of Scotland · Edinburgh · 2007

A CONTEMPORARY
PORTRAIT OF SCOTLAND'S
POLICE
PHOTOGRAPHS BY
JANE BRETTLE

PREVIOUS PAGE
**1 AIR SUPPORT UNIT**
STRATHCLYDE POLICE

The Air Support Unit provides aerial support to territorial divisions in the Strathclyde Police area. Strathclyde Police currently operate an EC135 T1 aircraft, and the unit is the only police helicopter service in Scotland. The unit is located at the Glasgow Heliport and the aircraft and crew are available seven days a week, 365 days a year. The unit covers an area of 5,348 sq. miles, a population of two and a half million people, and, at over 4,000 miles, a coastline greater than that of France. The unit has three operational crews made up of seven full-time officers; the unit executive officer, one sergeant and five constables. All crew members volunteer for the job and must maintain competency in fire fighting, first aid, underwater escape training and a variety of other skills. Any police officer is at liberty to request aerial support and the unit regularly responds to requests from police forces outside the Strathclyde area.

The captions that accompany the photographs were written by the officers portrayed in them.

# FOREWORD

The police are involved in many aspects of our daily life: from traffic control to mountain rescue; from drug enforcement to community support. Visible or invisible, the police touch our lives in more ways than we imagine.

*Force: A Contemporary Portrait of Scotland's Police* was commissioned by the Scottish National Portrait Gallery, to reflect the activities of the service the length and breadth of the country. It is the latest project in the Gallery's programme of commissions to show aspects of life in contemporary Scotland.

When the exhibition has finished its run at the Portrait Gallery, it will travel around Scotland. It has been made by Jane Brettle, whose most recent project, *airside*, is a series of large-scale photographic portraits of professional women who are innovators in their fields. Jane has visited all eight police forces in Scotland, recording the activities of a very wide range of police officers and their duties. For this she has had the full co-operation of the Scottish police themselves. Her work, it is important to remember, is an artist's impression of a body of professional men and women and as such is informed by the work of the great masters of the past.

Both Jane Brettle and the Scottish National Portrait Gallery would like to record their thanks to the many people involved in setting up this project and to the participants themselves for providing statements describing their work, which add greatly to the interest of the exhibition and this publication. They would like to thank both Amanda Hopkinson for her perceptive essay, which sets the photographs in their artistic context, and Louise Jackson for her informative essay on policing in modern Scotland. They wish to acknowledge the support of Eastern Digital Imaging in printing the photographs. Finally, the Scottish National Portrait Gallery is very grateful for the financial support to this project from the University of Northumbria and from Scottish Executive through Arts & Business.

**John Leighton**
*Director-General, National Galleries of Scotland*

**James Holloway**
*Director, Scottish National Portrait Gallery*

**2 DETECTIVE SERGEANT
DAVID NOLAN**
COMPUTER CRIME UNIT
CENTRAL SCOTLAND POLICE

The Computer Crime Unit (CCU) is responsible for investigating high-tech crimes. We forensically examine computers and peripherals such as USB keys, floppy discs, CDs, DVDs and mobile phones, which have been seized by officers. The unit is made up of two forensic analysts and two detectives and was formed in 2003 in response to Operation Ore, which was a worldwide investigation of users of websites featuring child pornography. Central Scotland Police received a number of paedophile targets from the FBI and after carrying out these investigations it was decided that there was a need for a dedicated unit to investigate high-tech crimes. The core business of the unit is the protection of children within police force boundaries and across the globe. A number of paedophiles across the world have been traced as a direct result of our operations. The unit also investigates the production and distribution of counterfeit DVDs and CDs. The majority of the criminals producing these discs are also producing and distributing hardcore pornography.

# INTRODUCTION
## LOUISE A. JACKSON

Every portrait is partial and unique. A likeness frozen in time and space, captured from a particular perspective, comments on a subject's distinctive features. In this exhibition, photographer Jane Brettle takes as her subject the men and women who, together, constitute the police service in Scotland. By setting images alongside each other, she creates a dynamic between individual officers, allegiances to local forces, and a wider collective occupational role, encouraging us to reflect on what it is that is distinctive about policing in Scotland.

Force identities have been shaped by the redrawing of boundaries and by their specific geographical, demographic and economic constituencies. The first 'modern' Scottish police forces were established in Glasgow in 1800, Edinburgh in 1805 and Aberdeen in 1815, pre-dating English equivalents (London's Metropolitan Police was founded in 1829). By 1859 there were thirty-two county constabularies and fifty-seven burgh forces in Scotland. These separate forces were gradually amalgamated to form ever larger administrative entities. The reorganisation of 1975 created the eight Scottish police forces of today: Central Scotland; Dumfries and Galloway; Fife; Grampian; Lothian and Borders; Northern; Strathclyde; and Tayside.

The regions they serve have contrasting characteristics. Northern Constabulary, which covers the Highlands and Islands, has a population density of less than eight people per square kilometre and, although one of the smallest police forces in the UK in numerical terms, bills itself as 'the safest' in terms of reported crime levels. The Strathclyde area includes Glasgow with a density of over 3,000 people per square kilometre; here the tackling of violent and drug-related crime is viewed as a priority to create a safer city. Human interaction with the local landscape and environment also shape the contours of Scottish policing. Wildlife officers in individual forces deal with the illegal poaching, trapping and killing of birds or animals, working in partnership with other organisations. Three forces maintain their own mountain rescue teams, whilst Grampian uniquely operates an Oil Industry Liaison Unit to police offshore installations.

Responsibility for operational policing is devolved to individual forces. Yet policy is formulated nationally through the Scottish Executive and Scottish Parliament. A strategic vision for the Scottish Police Service as a whole is co-ordinated through the Association of Chief Police Officers in Scotland (ACPOS). A range of services – including the Scottish Police College (at Tulliallan) and the Scottish Criminal Record Office – are centralised, whilst specialist support units (forensic science, air support and underwater search teams) are provided across forces. Delivery may be local, but policing in Scotland is shaped by national, UK-wide and global agendas including current concerns about international security.

Contemporary policing is a response to a complex past as well as to the present. From the late 1960s onwards, a series of complaints, inquiries and reports drew attention to incidents of police corruption, aggressive tactics and racism, creating a crisis in public confidence that was felt across the UK (although Scotland did not experience the inner city riots that took place in England). The overtly political use that was made of mobile police squads under the Thatcher administration during the miners' strike of 1984 became a point of concern for civil rights activists. The twenty-first century has subsequently seen an extensive repackaging of policing and an engagement with the concept of community to rebuild trust through an emphasis on the ethos of public service.

The terms 'force' and 'service' may appear as uneasy bedfellows. If 'force' suggests an imposition of will through strength, to 'serve' implies obedience, duty, deference to others and, in relation to the public sector, an ethic of care over control. When balanced in a perfect equilibrium they represent the pact that is struck within liberal democracies: the protection of collective 'community' interest through law enforcement. Scotland's police chiefs have laid out their priorities for the new century in a strategy document that emphasises the traditional aim of policing to 'prevent and detect crime and to preserve public order'. They also state that 'the underlying themes of community reassurance and community well-being will underpin the priorities, as developing safer communities must remain the primary objective that drives policing activity' (ACPOS, Policing Priorities for Scotland 2006–9). Policing within, on behalf of, and in partnership with the local community is stressed consistently in the language of contemporary policing, a trend that developed in Scotland from the 1970s.

The need to serve a community that is constituted through diversity is also emphasised in strategy and policy. Yet the operational face of policing is still overwhelmingly white and male. In the wake of the Macpherson Report on the enquiry into the murder of Stephen Lawrence in 1999, the Scottish Executive set up a steering group to examine racial discrimination within Scottish policing. Since then Scottish police forces have developed diversity strategies and set up diversity units to promote trust and to deal with hate crimes relating to race or sexual orientation. Yet, ethnic minorities are still under-represented in Scottish police forces, forming only around two per cent of police officers in Strathclyde (although thirty-one per cent of Scotland's ethnic minority population lives in Glasgow). Following the Sexual Discrimination Act of 1975 women have been employed in policing on the same terms and conditions as men. In 2003 they constituted nineteen per cent of police officers in Scotland. Only two women are currently members of ACPOS: the Director of the Scottish Police College, Margaret Barr, and the Deputy Chief Constable of Fife Constabulary, Norma Graham. By forming their own associations to promote diversity within policing – the Gender Agenda Committee, SEMPERscotland, and the Gay Police Association – rank and file officers are campaigning

**3 COMMUNITY SUPPORT UNIT**
LOTHIAN AND BORDERS POLICE

The Community Support Unit (CSU) forms part of the Operations Division within Lothian and Borders Police. The unit is based at force headquarters and consists of two inspectors, five sergeants and twenty-three constables – these personnel make up three teams, each led by a sergeant. The teams are responsible for providing specialist support to the force. The CSU provides support across many areas of expertise including counter-terrorism search teams, missing persons search managers and advisors, chemical, biological, radiological and nuclear support and training, photographic evidence gathering at public events, public order issues and tactical matters related to spontaneous incidents and pre-planned public events and marine unit officers responsible for waterborne policing and incidents.

for change. The aspiration that policing should reflect the needs of a diverse community is indicated here in the image of PC Wendy Blair of the Asylum Liaison Unit in Glasgow [Plate 6].

As an outsider looking in, Brettle's method for creating a portrait of contemporary Scottish policing involved dialogue with members of each force, asking them in turn what they felt was distinctive about their role. Each force suggested individuals, groups and areas of work as possible focal points for her images. Decisions about where and what to photograph were negotiated between Brettle and her subjects. There is no one image of policing in Scotland that can convey the breadth and range of activity. Policing has become increasingly professionalised over the last thirty years as the number of specialist roles, all involving extensive training, has grown substantially. Arguably, here, the ordinary uniformed constable engaged in general operations is under-represented. Yet, the sense of the everyday is maintained in the portrait of Scott Haig, the only police officer on the Shetland island of Unst [Plate 12], or in the image of dog handler Alan Murray, at home with his family [Plate 20]. All officers are involved in general operations during the course of their service and may return to it after specialist duties.

The development of policing and photography have gone hand in glove. In its early days it was assumed that photography unproblematically recorded a scientific and instantaneous 'truth' in the form of visible fact. Its ability to capture visual likeness was quickly made use of in policing. Fox Talbot is credited with the 'invention' of a practical (or viable) positive/negative process in 1840; within ten years Birmingham City Police had become the first force to make use of photographic portraits in criminal records. By the 1880s the mugshot had been standardised as a key means of recording the identity of convicted offenders and prisoners; a mirror was placed behind the subject's head at an angle of forty-five degrees to capture both a side and full-face profile. Photographic records of all released prisoners were shared across Scotland's

**4 SPECIAL PC TREVOR KILLEN**
RADIO OPERATIONS, RAF KINLOSS
GRAMPIAN CONSTABULARY

My role as a special constable is varied but usually involves regular operational policing, mostly at the weekends when resources can be stretched. I am on duty every other weekend and give one night per month to training. The work is varied and challenging and affords me the opportunity to put something back to my local community.

police forces by the 1890s. If photographic portraiture could capture the 'truth' or essence of an individual, could it not also reveal further 'truths' about the capacity for criminality? In 1877 scientist Francis Galton began an analysis of around 600 photographic portraits of convicts, aiming to build up a composite image of the criminal 'type' (his findings remained inconclusive).

In terms of police method a clear distinction must be made between the use of photography to identify a specific 'type' and the use of photography to identify particular individuals. Innovations in the use of forensic photography were developed by Glasgow police, after a Fingerprinting and Photography Department was introduced to the city in 1931. Glasgow officers worked in conjunction with John Glaister Senior and John Glaister Junior, both professors of forensic medicine at the University of Glasgow. The Glaisters experimented with X-ray and ultraviolet photography as well as photomicrography, which allowed them to show the distinguishing features in an individual hair. The photographic gaze, once again, could reveal the inner 'truth' about identity.

Increasing amounts of personal information about convicted offenders – including images – were collected from the nineteenth century onwards. Yet it is only within the last few decades that the computing technology has existed to systematically process, manage and search data. Portrait photographs are stored as digitised images held in a central database and it is also possible to mount electronic identification parades (VIPER), which make use of video techniques. The technological revolution of the late twentieth century has transformed police surveillance from physical patrol of fixed beats to sophisticated forms of electronic information collation. Similarly video surveillance (CCTV) has led to forms of 'virtual' policing, with police operational time spent, instead, on image analysis. Moreover, information technology and the ease of circulating digital images have led to 'new' forms of crime as well as their detection.

The police have been more likely to make use

of photographs of others than to photograph themselves. Historically, there have been moments when the police have actively resisted the gaze of photography, most obviously during the miners' strike when activists claimed that personal identifiers such as numbers were removed from uniforms. When they have represented themselves, the police have rarely drawn attention to notions of individuality. The formal team photograph – including the training school photo, which marks a rite of passage for each distinct cohort of new constables – is linked to group performance, identity and camaraderie. The publicity photograph, produced within the service for wider popular consumption – to promote policing as a career choice or to relay positive messages about the social value of the service – focuses on the occupation of the police officer rather than its meaning in terms of the individual. The aim of the police uniform itself is to erode personal distinctions to create an instantly recognisable and ubiquitous police identity. Official portraits of police officers as individuals, as in many other occupations, have been used as a format reserved for the most senior ranks and as an accord of high achievement.

Brettle's images of serving police officers reference these familiar ways of representing the police alongside other traditions of formal portraiture. Yet her images also challenge the assumptions that underpin our understanding of the familiar as she combines these allusions in fresh ways, drawing the viewer into a dialogue. In approaching one of her photographs we might begin by asking obvious questions about work role as we look for conventional indicators provided by specialist uniform and equipment. Then we look further. We might be drawn to ask questions about the social relationships that link individuals within a group. In some cases, too, the image itself relays an intimacy that indicates the highly personal and subjective engagement of an officer with his or her work. Whilst policing is often viewed in terms of public roles, the theme of domestic space resonates through many of the images. The emotional work that policing may entail is suggested in the images of the officers involved in child protection, family liaison, and work with the families of the Lockerbie victims. The meaning of each image is not fixed by the camera lens but is located in the moment of meeting between subject, photographer and, crucially, viewer. Ultimately Brettle leads us to draw our own conclusions about the significance of policing in twenty-first century Scotland.

*Dr Louise A. Jackson is Lecturer in Economic & Social History, School of History and Classics, University of Edinburgh.*

# FORCE: PHOTOGRAPHS BY JANE BRETTLE
## AMANDA HOPKINSON

Five years after the millennium, the G-8 summit was held in Scotland. In the centre of Edinburgh, clashes took place at the very entrance to the great red sandstone Victorian edifice of the Scottish National Portrait Gallery, home to the images of the most famous people in Scottish history along with the battles they fought. A sensation of image and reality confronting each other must have crossed the threshold, as the Director of the Portrait Gallery, James Holloway was later to remark: 'That day I was very much aware of the police for the first time in my life. They were literally on the doorstep, I thought "what an interesting subject. I don't really know what they do." It seemed perfect for our programme of displays reflecting aspects of contemporary Scotland.'

It was a logical choice for James Holloway to approach photographer Jane Brettle, who had previously shown and published two major exhibitions of portraits in Edinburgh. The first of these, *Venus Rising* put her work in the context of Titian's *Venus Anadyomene*. These works, a series of six diptychs titled *Restoration Works*, 2002, place five of possibly the most famous sculptures in the western world by the Italian 'master of marble', Canova, beside portraits of women in modest approximations of the stances of *The Three Graces, Venus, Psyche, Letizia* and *Paolina Bonaparte*. The mind's eye insists on comparing and contrasting what the images specifically avert: the real and the ideal; the modern and the classical; the inner world of the museum and the urban context of the contemporary backgrounds. Brettle's women are as deliberately in situ – in their knowing poses, in their various collegiate and urban surroundings – as the gleaming marble statues are in their pillared halls hung with nineteenth-century landscapes.

Brettle's subsequent exhibition and catalogue, called *airside*, 2003, assumes seriously its mission to 'reconsider portrait painting through the contemporary medium of photography and digital imaging'. This time the act of repositioning does not take place through diptychs, but through a series of solo portraits taken 'to celebrate the contribution of twenty-eight women from very different worlds to her own… who are making a substantial contribution to life and culture'. None the less, these are, again, characteristic Brettle portraits: large (up to 150 × 110 cm) colour prints of women taken face on, unsmiling – though sometimes unserious – always intently, into the camera. Again, clothes and content are balanced in significance with attitude and expression: each single image is an intentional summary of a life's achievement, a statement of not only *who* the sitter is, but *where* she is at this point in time. This contextualisation connects to what Brettle likes to describe as the 'skins' which we all wear in crossing the personal with the professional – and none of us more so than women aware of being among the first of our kind in a given career.

Perhaps the pedigree of these two 'in-depth investigations' resonated with the police; a profession more accustomed to undertaking their own enquires. Perhaps it was the coolness of Brettle's gaze, levelly returned by the subjects who meet hers as equals. If the portrait is impeccable, it is the detached look of the artist that remains inscrutable. Clearly, however, she is concerned with at least two things: the minority that makes a difference (whether school girls or high-achieving woman professionals); and the context in which they are framed.

All portraiture involves the collaboration of the sitter. Historically, painted miniatures were used as a medium of communication for lovers and enemies alike. The intended message was frequently more than the visual information contained. Henry VIII's fury at the lack of actual resemblance between the painted flattery he was sent to introduce him to Anne of Cleves and the 'mare of Flanders' he personally met when his betrothed came to Hampton Court is still currency. Jane Brettle, however, was anxious '… not to be accused of collaboration or flattery. I need to get the subjects to understand what I do as an artist.'

Unusually among many of her profession, Brettle is unabashed at thus describing herself as an artist, and her work has more in common with a particular period of art than with the general medium of photography. She acknowledges the influence of the Golden Age of Dutch group portraiture and the paintings of Holbein, in which the inner world of the subject is reflected in the everyday, secular world in which they are placed. Indeed, Brettle chose as a contributor to her previous catalogue Joanna Woodall, deputy director of London's Courtauld Institute, whose specialism is Netherlandish Art of the Early Modern period.[1] Small wonder, then, at the explicit comparisons between her field of interest and Brettle's. No surprise, either, that when Jane and I meet, in January 2007, she describes seeking 'painterly quality with a clear depth of field…' and refers to the *texture* of pixels as reminiscent of oil pigment, and to the way in which she makes the work as akin to standing before an easel.

This tradition has far more association with her work than that of postwar 'humanitarian' photography, dependent on natural accident, the coincidence of individual and situation, the camera roving abroad, capturing a passing smile and people on the move. A world the camera is supposed not to deceive but only to record. To which the one possible response is that of course the camera, being a machine, does not either lie or tell the truth; it's the photographer, being human, who chooses to do so. Brettle's chosen instrument is a fixed plate Hasselblad, digitally adapted, that belongs to an altogether earlier period – arguably to that of the high art – of photographic portraiture. Until the invention of a practical (or viable) negative/positive process in 1840, portraiture was a matter of long sittings and slow exposures; head and waist braces; and no smiles. Something about the deliberation was intended, in the famous phrase of pioneer Victorian portraitist Julia Margaret Cameron, to allow for the contemplation she described in the famous quote: 'When I have had such men before my camera, my whole soul has endeavoured to do its duty towards them in recording faithfully the greatness of the inner as

**5 NATIONAL SUPPORT STAFF**
LOTHIAN AND BORDERS POLICE

Tricia Cochrane is the equal opportunities and diversity adviser for Lothian and Borders Police and is concerned with gender, disability, race, age, sexual orientation, and religion and belief within the police force. Nationally, she is on the Women's Development Forum committee and chairs the Disability Awareness Focus Group and Gender Equality Group and she is one of two Scottish representatives on the British Association of Women in Policing committee. Inspector Dinesh Joshi joined Lothian and Borders Police as its first Indian officer thirty years ago. He was the first vice-chairperson for SEMPERscotland (which supports staff in police service). He has been involved extensively in race-relations work and was awarded an MBE in 2002 for his contribution to this area. He currently sits on several committees and is the secretary of the Edinburgh Indian Association. Inspector David Lyle has served in Lothian and Borders Police for twenty-five years. He became the Scottish co-ordinator for the Gay Police Association in 1998. Since April 2006, he has worked on a full-time basis on behalf of gay and bisexual people in all eight Scottish police forces.

well as the features of the outer man.'²

This faith was frequently ill-rewarded by the inability of the sitter to transcend the tedium and discomfort of the necessarily lengthy sessions demanded by early 'box' cameras with brass screw-on lenses, heavy as a ship's telescope; particularly when imposed by a photographer as bossy as Cameron herself. Brettle refuses to enter into the paradox whereby the photographer's determination to obtain a specific outcome elicits spontaneity from the subject. In the first letter she wrote to me inviting my participation, in October 2006, she repeatedly uses the adjective 'objective'. 'My aim has been to be objective in relation to the choice of subjects. After working my way around all eight forces for the first three months of 2006, I felt that the best approach both from my own interest and from an audience point of view was to ask each force how they felt they were unique.'³ In this instance, 'Uniqueness embraces difference in geography, population density and community, as well as certain specialisations.'

Having previously explored issues around 'the gendered language of architecture',⁴ Brettle was now to revisit her adoptive homeland and reconstruct it geographically along the lines which an essentially masculine 'force' had divided into unequal eighths – from the vast northern distances to the intensity of inner-city policing – for ease of administration. She was to see the country anew and spend three winter months visiting the recently-reformed forces across the country, from Shetland to the Borders, the west coast to the Solway Firth, Glasgow to Tayside. Unwilling to be co-opted into a propaganda exercise, she found 'the Force' (as they call themselves) willing to co-operate in making the necessary arrangements without stipulating parameters. 'I wanted their subjectivity to define the work rather than to impose my own.'

Brettle's manner of working, based on a capacity for meticulous preparation and phenomenal attention to detail combined with her encompassing vision alludes to a capacity for seeing beyond

**6 PC WENDY BLAIR**
ASYLUM LIAISON UNIT
STRATHCLYDE POLICE

I am a police constable with Strathclyde Police and have fifteen years service. I am attached to the Asylum Liaison Unit in Glasgow. This division, which plays host to around 6,000 asylum seekers and the vast majority of the 3,000 or so refugees living in Glasgow, is the only one in Strathclyde with a dedicated unit dealing with asylum and refugee issues, and racially aggravated crime. My gender has enabled me to overcome cultural barriers and I am actively involved with black and minority ethnic women within the community. There is still inherent mistrust of the police, many believing any contact with them will affect asylum claims. I regularly meet with key individuals to discuss areas of concern. Many of these women would never dream of approaching the police or entering a police office so meetings are held in a local church. Areas of discussion can range from not having a working smoke alarm, to concerns about drugs. Through successfully tackling the smaller issues, the community feels encouraged to report more serious matters.

edges of the frame, and helped to establish her reputation for creative synergy. This fitted well within the genre of Scottish portraiture as newly defined by the Scottish National Portrait Gallery's commitment to more popular subjects. English by birth, Jane Brettle has lived the greater part of her life in Scotland, and has the essential prerequisites of both her long familiarity with the land and with portraiture.

It is an old anthropological device to give 'primitive' peoples samples of their image, then to get them to bring to the photo-session examples of what they hold dear. That way, it was believed (from the nineteenth century until at least the 1940s) the subjects would not feel 'robbed' of their image (and so their soul), since they still retained control over the first imprint. A century and a half's-worth of albums have been filled with portraits of 'natives' in far-flung or unfamiliar territories (i.e. unfamiliar at the time to western explorers and investigators) bearing their implements for hunting, cooking, building, sewing and making artefacts. Women most often come accompanied by their children. What started as a trick of a new medium fast became normal practice.

Thus while the police would not have seen themselves as under 'objective' investigation, they went for the exhibition of the tools of their trade, as well as the foregrounding of their community work, particularly with members of minorities and victims of sexual aggression. Many unexpected barriers are crossed, as indicated by the portrait of Inspector David Lyle, Scottish co-ordinator of the Gay Police Association, seated beneath a wall of shields, together with his colleagues, Inspector Dinesh Joshi, awarded an MBE for his work with ethnic minorities in the Lothian and Borders Police and Tricia Cochrane of the Women's Development Forum [plate 5]. Or PC Wendy Blair of Strathclyde Police's Asylum Liaison Unit, seated at a church hall table – carefully spread with a check tablecloth, a tray of plastic cups, a vase containing red and yellow flowers – in company with local

### 7 POLICE FORENSIC SCIENCE LABORATORY
TAYSIDE POLICE

Our aim is to impartially inform intelligence and assist justice through science. The Police Forensic Science Laboratory (PFSLD) has a staff of seventy-three people spread across several main sections. The Biology Section identifies and DNA-profiles blood and other body fluids and undertakes blood pattern and damage interpretation on items of clothing, weapons and material recovered from crime scenes. The Chemistry Section analyses unidentified powders and substances in relation to the Misuse of Drugs Act, undertakes paint and glass comparisons, general chemistry and fire investigation including analysis of fire debris for accelerants. The DNA Database Section manages the Scottish DNA Database. This involves DNA profiling of mouth swabs and comparison with crime scene profiles. This can identify a link between a person and a crime scene or link a series of crimes. The section also undertakes criminal paternity and human remains identification nationally. Intelligence-led screens are also undertaken using mouth swabs from volunteers. These screens assist police trying to identify or eliminate individuals as the source of crime-connected DNA. The section also undertakes criminal paternity and human remains identification nationally.

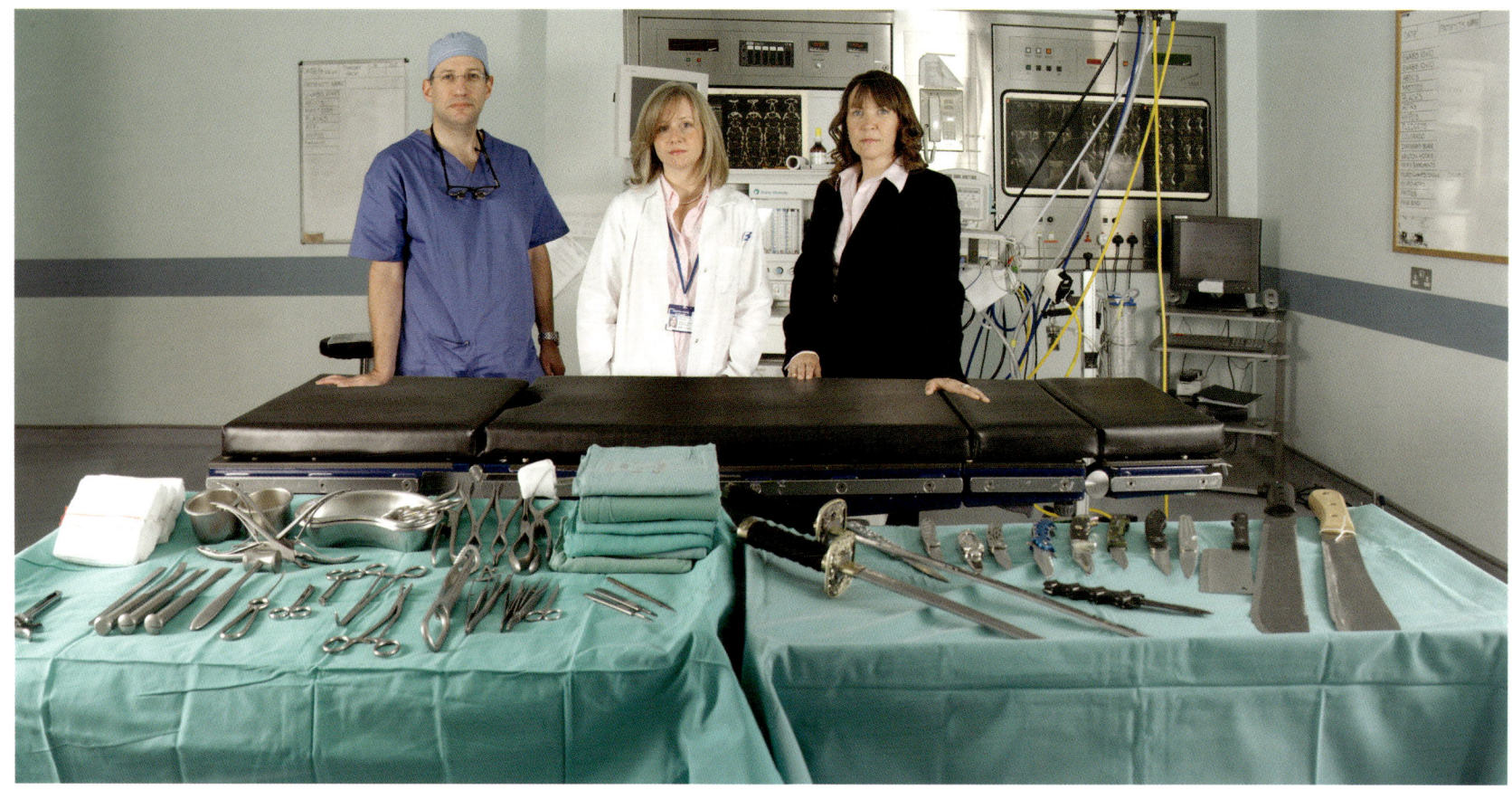

**8** VIOLENCE REDUCTION UNIT
STRATHCLYDE POLICE

The Violence Reduction Unit (VRU) was established by Strathclyde Police in January 2005 to reduce violence, particularly knife crime. Violence in Scotland is a chronic problem with little change in the pattern since the 1930s. Glasgow has the highest rate of murder in Europe, and murders committed with a knife are three and a half times higher than that of England and Wales. The World Health Organisation report on violence, 2002, highlights Scotland as having a homicide rate similar to Argentina, Costa Rica and Lithuania. Murders in Scotland are the tip of the iceberg; an increasing volume of attempted murders, serious and simple assaults and a culture of knife carrying has persisted despite concerted efforts by the police during repeated enforcement operations. Working with hospitals and many others, the VRU is approaching violence as a public health problem, and it aspires to change the culture of violent behaviour in Scotland.

**9** PC KEITH MULLOY
SCHOOL BASED POLICE OFFICER
GRAMPIAN POLICE

In August 2002 Grampian Police and Northfield Academy in Aberdeen, entered into a unique partnership by creating a school based police officer (SBO) who is part of a multi-agency team, the first of its kind in Scotland. As the SBO I am a fully operational police officer based within the school. I provide support and advice to young people and their families in the Northfield area and assist the school in efforts to reduce truancy, bullying, anti-social behaviour and crime within the school and its community. Along with school staff, I work closely with young people to channel their behaviour. I arrange activities such as art projects, in an attempt to challenge and reduce vandalism; outdoor education, which offers pupils learning experiences in a different environment; and pedal cycle projects to improve pupil confidence, road safety, cycle skills and cycle maintenance.

**10 MOUNTED SECTION**
LOTHIAN AND BORDERS POLICE

Horses have been used to combat crime in Britain since 1758. Currently seventeen UK police forces use horses. The seven Lothian and Borders horses carry out work as diverse as leading civic parades, searching open countryside for missing people, patrolling city streets and attending community events. The horses are chosen for their patience and bravery and come from diverse backgrounds. The smallest, Scout, is 16.2 hands high and the tallest, Fife, is 18.2 hands high (the tallest police horse in the UK). Commander (left) is the leader of the group and a steadying influence. He and his rider have a strong bond – so much so that when his rider is away Commander broods. Merlin is more capricious – he's always looking for the next practical joke to play.

Muslims [plate 6]. Wendy Blair is the only woman working in the group of three officers in the Asylum Liaison Unit in Glasgow, where over fifty-two different mother tongues are spoken in primary schools in the area around the Red Road football ground. The irony, leavened with hospitality, of such a heterogeneous group (on this occasion all Turkish, some in European dress; one in the shawal-kameez) seated beneath a cross, beside that most British of institutions, the teapot, is belied by the manner in which even the young boy looks into camera with unassuming warmth.

Perhaps more unexpectedly, women compose three-quarters of the chemical biologists working in forensics. In a tableau reminiscent of Rembrandt's *'Anatomy Lesson'*, where the medics' gaze is directed away from the corpse they are dissecting, and where every instrument and text is carefully positioned, the forensics team are shown, in their latex gloves and white overalls, likewise frozen in time [plate 7]. Their gaze is directed outwards through their protective eyewear as their hands busy themselves, unsupervised, with opening bottles, taking a swab, sterilising a cotton drape, writing entries in a ledger. The accompanying triptych shows the team at work collecting samples from the floor dressed in all-enveloping protective clothing; members of the unit presenting the evidence at a podium; and then – suddenly office workers just like most of us – seated before their computers at the DNA database centre. The disquieting interface between crime and medicine is made even more explicit in the portrait of three collaborators aiming to reduce violence in Strathclyde. Consultant David Koppel apparently prepares to perform a dissection behind a table showing an array of gleaming stainless steel surgical instruments [plate 8]. Beside him are two young women, one Dr Christine Goodall in a white coat, the other, Karyn McCluskey of Strathclyde Police's Violence Reduction Unit in a dark suit. They stand at an identical surgical table spread with a bright turquoise sheet, as if to offset the impact of its battery of machetes, stilettos, cleavers, axes, even

**11 ACTING SERGEANT PHILIP JOHNSTONE AND PC NEIL GRAHAM**
COMMUNITY POLICE OFFICERS
DUMFRIES AND GALLOWAY
CONSTABULARY

On 13 February 2006, the cockle beds on the Solway Firth in south-west Scotland were opened up for cockle fishing. The large number of people who descended on the small village of Powfoot near Annan to fish for cockles resulted in community concerns that the cocklers were putting themselves in danger by going on to the Solway Firth. The influx of cocklers also impacted on the quality of life of the residents of Powfoot who, until then, had not experienced this type of activity. Although legislation relating to cockle fishing rests with other agencies, local police officers still have an important role to play. Community police officers based within the Community Policing Unit at Annan Police Station carried out foot and cycle patrols to reassure the community and to provide a deterrent to would-be criminals. The cockle beds opened again on 13 December 2006 and police officers carried out high visibility patrols along the Solway coast. Community police officers on pedal cycles are at the forefront of these patrols.

**12** PC SCOTT HAIG
NORTHERN CONSTABULARY

Unst is the most northerly-inhabited island within the Shetland Isles, with a population of around 600 people made up of locals and incomers. The island has an extremely close-knit community, which is largely free from bias and intolerance. Community involvement is the backbone of successfully policing the island and there is an expectation from the community that I should always be available. People often arrive at the house seeking help (often out of hours). My role on the island is to offer reassurance as well as to deal with the numerous challenges expected of the police, from investigating and reporting crime to road accidents, firearm enquiries and community liaison through talks at local schools, care centres and local groups. I have no anonymity as I am based on such a small island. Whether in uniform or out I am always viewed as a police officer and because of this it can sometimes be difficult to gain the trust of locals and put them at ease during social events.

**13** INSPECTOR IAN REID
ROYALTY AND VIP
PLANNING UNIT
GRAMPIAN POLICE

Inspector Ian Reid is the officer-in-charge of the Royalty and VIP Planning Unit based at the Operational Planning Department in Aberdeen. The unit, formed in 1991, is responsible for developing and co-ordinating all aspects of Royalty and VIP protection within Grampian Police. Major Hutton is the officer commanding the Royal Guard, A Company, The Highlanders (Seaforth, Gordons and Camerons), 4th Battalion, the Royal Regiment of Scotland. The Royal Guard provides support to the police security operation during Her Majesty The Queen's residence at Balmoral. During the period of the Royal Court, between early August and early October each year, when Her Majesty and other members of the Royal Family are in residence on Deeside, Grampian Police work in partnership with the Balmoral Estates, the Metropolitan Police Service and the Royal Guard to ensure the safety of the Royal Family.

two swords. Behind them is a mass of blue and yellow cables as if belonging to a life support machine; beside them is a luminous X-ray screen.

Triptychs recur, for example, in the role play exercises of the Forensic Laboratory [plate 7] and at the Police Training College [back cover]. Something about the format, forever associated with high altars in medieval churches, belonging to a period when they were the religious cartoon strips of the day, runs through the teaching medium here too. The consciously didactic aspect of contemporary police work is not overlooked either: in Grampian, PC Keith Mulloy goes to work in a school, where he has an office [plate 9]. However, his job is not to stay in it, but to participate in the classroom, and to serve as a bridge between school and the wider community. On the wall is pinned a list of terms for marijuana – dope, weed, ganja, etc – over one of the coloured circles intersected with geometric shapes that comprise the more usual art room decoration. A group of pupils are applying themselves to designing posters warning of the consequences of its consumption.

The less cuddly aspect of police work has, as in the events surrounding the G-8 summit, to do with 'preserving law and order'. Jane Brettle is not slow to pick up on the innate conservatism of such a message, while again insisting that it has nothing to do with either political propaganda or public censorship. The potentially threatening aspect of two members of the Lothian and Borders mounted police is mitigated by the photographer choosing to place each officer facing their unsaddled steeds, one without her helmet, in the green setting of a summery day in the park [plate 10]. The horses are straight out of a George Stubbs painting: at least seventeen hands high, standing squarely to attention, necks aligned, coats gleaming, and only their gentle gaze at their riders softening the overall majesty of their stance. This is the only portrait where the attributes have overtaken the protagonists, and where the police officers are looking away from the camera.

As if in parody, two community officers from

## 14 FOOTBALL MATCH COMMANDS
### E AND G DIVISIONS, STRATHCLYDE POLICE

In the west of Scotland, within a ten-mile radius, there are three major football stadiums – Ibrox Stadium and Celtic Park, and Hampden the National Stadium – each commanding home crowds in excess of 50,000. The safety of spectators attending football matches and other large-scale events lies with the match commander assisted by his Operational Planning Team. In addition to this core group, strong partnerships have to exist between the police and various other agencies including Glasgow City Council, Strathclyde Ambulance Service and, of course, the clubs themselves. Chief Superintendent Kenny Scott (E Division) and Chief Superintendent Robin Howe (G Division) are both match commanders. Superintendent Alex McAllister and Superintendent Andy Bates act as their deputies. Chief Superintendent Scott has policing responsibility for Celtic Park and also acts as a security adviser to UEFA. Chief Superintendent Howe has responsibility for both Ibrox Stadium and the National Stadium – the venues for thirty-eight football matches in the 2005–6 season, with an attendance of 1.6 million people.

**15 PC JEFF ADAMS**
DIVING SUPERVISOR
UNDERWATER SEARCH UNIT
CENTRAL SCOTLAND POLICE

The unit has been in existence since 1962 and is one of only three such units, covering the whole of Scotland. There are two full-time staff and eight part-time. A dive team normally consists of six officers. Diving operations are carried out to recover people who have drowned; stolen or lost property; crashed vehicles and items used in crimes such as weapons and tools. Anything that is submerged – from jewellery to aircraft wreckage – can become the object of a search. The unit also carries out boat patrols, confined space searches in locations such as sewers, anti-terrorist searches, crime scene searches and water safety initiatives. One very successful safety initiative is our annual 'Crucial Crew' event at Bo'ness. This is a multi-agency event involving all of the emergency services and other volunteers. Over a two-week period we deliver hands-on water safety training to over 1,000 primary school children.

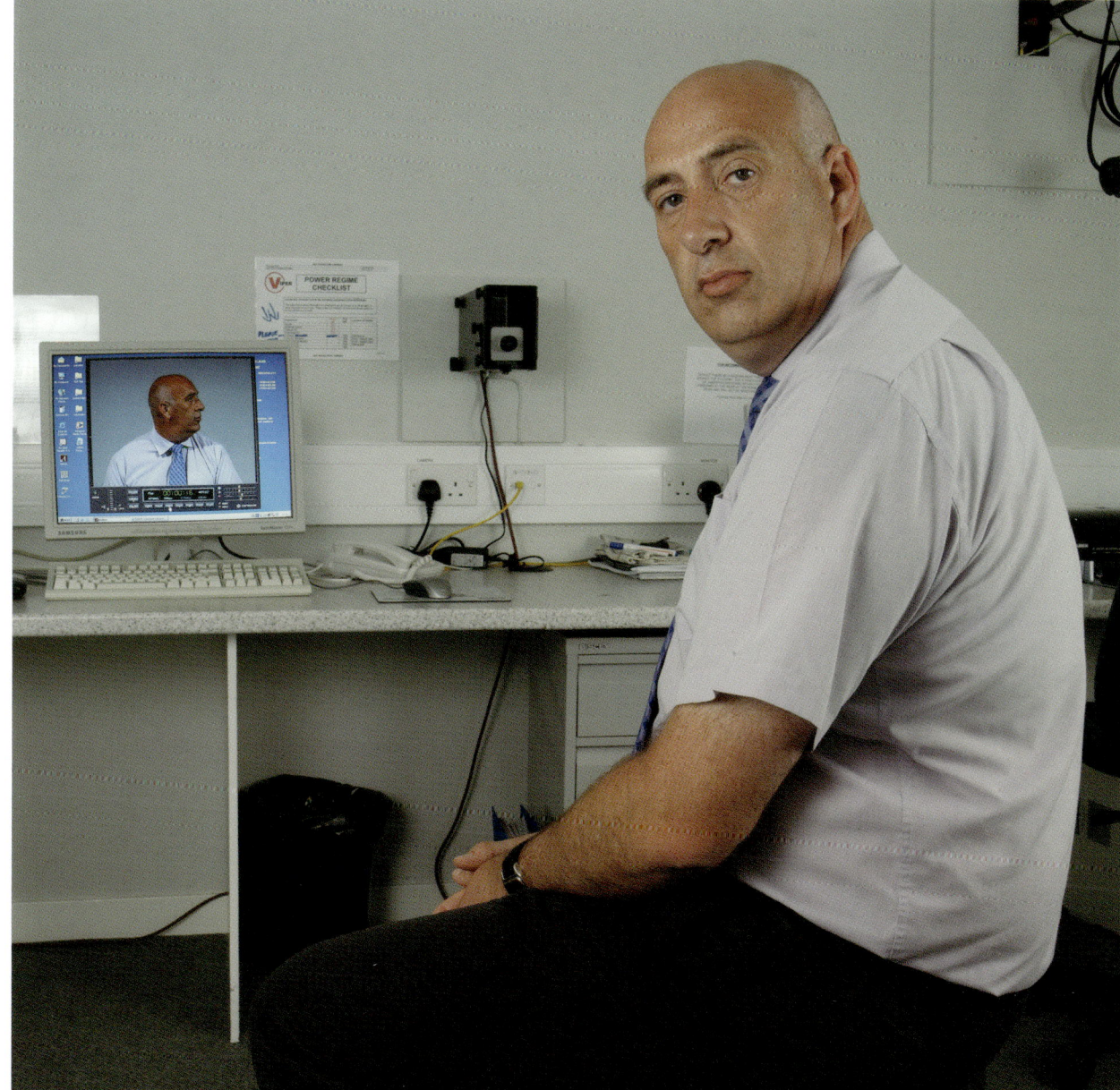

**16** DETECTIVE CONSTABLE
NEILL BINGHAM
CRIMINAL JUSTICE
DEPARTMENT
FIFE CONSTABULARY

The identification of a person accused of a crime is an essential element of any criminal proceeding. The Video Identification Parade Suite (VIPER) uses state-of-the-art video and computer technology to produce a virtual identification parade. The VIPER suite of Fife Constabulary is based at Kirkcaldy Police Station. Operators within Fife are responsible for all stages of the organisation, conduct and reporting of VIPER identification parades to the appropriate Procurator Fiscal. Video identification has been of great benefit to victims of crime because they no longer come into direct physical contact with the suspect. Witnesses can, in certain circumstances, take part in VIPER identification parades from their own homes, which helps the witness feel more at ease. Both the VIPER suite and its trained officers assist with enquiries from other police forces in Scotland, and from our English, Welsh and Irish colleagues.

Dumfries and Galloway are taken, pulled up on their bicycles, again facing each other **[plate 11]**. This time, however, the camera's look is returned, and the setting is not the tamed gardens of a park but the wilder shores of the grey and grizzled coastland, where their phosphorescent yellow jackets stand out unnatural in their brilliance. Further out and wilder, Mallaig is the setting for the Wildlife Crime Officer John Bryden, lined up with his tame eagle owl on his gauntlet, festooned with a chain and a bunch of keys **[front cover]**. Rare egg – even rare moth – stealing is a serious problem in the area, as is the dangerous and unregistered raiding of the pearl mussel beds: Bryden is tasked with attempting to reduce both. Man and bird stare straight into camera, as the mists descend over the mountains of Lochailort.

Still more remote is the home of Scott and Janette Haig and their two children, Lucy and Ross, up at Baltasound, on Unst, the most northerly of all the Shetland Isles **[plate 12]**. It is one of the very few pictures where one of the subjects is smiling. Janette's expression, so typical of the reflex smile of the snapshot – a photographic tradition that could hardly be further from Brettle's own – makes the group portrait seem like another genre altogether. In terms of its composition, only Scott's shoulder tabs and the police car in the family garage behind reveal it does not belong in a commonplace family album.

A certain self-referential humour is also, apparently, admissible. Inspector Ian Reid and Major Alex Hutton, the former in sober civvies, the latter (clearly a giant of a man) in khaki shirt and Gordon tartan kilt are seated on a leather sofa draped with a leopard skin **[plate 13]**. Such animal exotica well befits a military man returned from Iraq to perform the duties of a Queen's Guard at Balmoral; the proximity to plain clothes policing renders explicit the closeness of two British forces. The clashing aesthetics of the floral carpet and the gilded painting entitled *The 92nd Storming a Hill Fort in Afghanistan* at the Victoria Barracks in Ballater, Aberdeenshire, frame the pair top and bottom with a riot of pattern and colour. The portrait of Detective Constable Neill Bingham, a specialist in the Criminal Justice Department, shows him seated in the Video Identification Parade Suite in Kirkcaldy Police Station **[plate 16]**. Bingham fronts his own on-screen image, offering an encapsulated version of the history of mugshot photography – once so crucial in police identification parades.

The full list of photographs takes in a surprising amount of our play and the police's work. Strathclyde Police's Football Match Commands reprise a triptych format linking the concave panorama of the Hampden Park Stadium shortly before the Scottish Cup Final: truly a cathedral constructed for a contemporary Sunday congregation **[plate 14]**. Meanwhile, PC Jeff Adams, Diving Supervisor for the Central Scotland Underwater Search Unit, instructs a group of rapt schoolchildren in elementary life-saving on the edge of a misty loch **[plate 15]**. Without a caption, what would the viewer make of the tools of *his* training? They include, apparently, a football being weighed in the palm of one hand against a cola bottle in the other. And Inspector Graham Gibb stands behind a massive tangle of ropes, ice-picks, shovels, pitons, grappling irons, helmets and oilskins, as if relegated to the back of the room, pinned to the rear wall in the photo-gallery of his earlier escapades **[plate 17]**. Leader of the Operational Support Division at Braemar, Gibb is tasked to know every inch of the local terrain covered by the Mountain Rescue Team. A curious lateral link makes him a leading expert in the field of missing person behaviour profiling, a specialism, which, by contrast, takes him all over the world.

Toys – the traditional variety made of wood and including paper and crayons, with not an electronic gadget in sight – are in the foreground in the group portrait of Anita and Stuart Dow, together with their son, Lewis **[plate 18]**. Anita is a detective constable attached to the Amethyst Team, Lothian and Borders Police. The family could as well have been sitting in their living room or posing in a photo studio, an indication of how far policing has

**17 INSPECTOR GRAHAM GIBB MBE**
OPERATIONAL SUPPORT DIVISION
GRAMPIAN POLICE

Inspector Graham J. Gibb has completed thirty-one years service with Grampian Police. He has twenty-seven years mountain rescue experience, including twenty years as leader of the joint Grampian Police and Braemar Mountain Rescue Team. In 1996 he was honoured with an MBE for his services to mountain rescue. Over the years Graham has developed a personal interest in the behaviour of missing people and has published behavioural profiles for them, and is now a leading expert in the field of missing person 'Behaviour Profiling'. The Scottish Police Service is unique in that Tayside, Strathclyde and Grampian Police, maintain their own Police Mountain Rescue Teams, made up of serving police officers, who work closely with their local volunteer teams. There are fourteen officers in the Grampian Rescue Team and they have responsibility for some 500 square miles of mountainous terrain, including the Cairngorm National Park. They respond to some forty-five incidents annually. Winter rescues can take up to four days, often in extreme weather conditions.

been domesticated according to the demands of a family situation, however constructed. While Anita and Stuart permit themselves a half-smile at the lens, their child poses with his head partly tipped forward and eyes raised, Princess Diana-style.

Such comfort zone portraits alternate with what Brettle has called the 'scary' ones (as in: 'Once they get into action, it's quite scary, setting off flares and things') – those where policing becomes militarised. Members of the Lothian and Borders Firearms Support Unit appear behind a battery of weaponry, several in body armour, another in camouflage, always one in mufti **[plate 19]**. Those in helmets, masks and with full body shields for crowd control inevitably appear sinister and menacing. Beside them, Dog Handler Alan Murray in the bosom of his family **[plate 20]** and the CCTV control room of the Ports Authority (a different sort of team unit complete with sniffer dog) look tame, quaint and arguably old-fashioned **[plate 24]**. The two extremes – an arms parade for potential military deployment and a reliance on man's best friend – also present us with an historical spectrum of police work.

The force's own version of their history is referenced in the Maritime Museum at Aberdeen. As with the overarching architecture at Hampden Stadium, so here a genuine oil rig built through three floors of the building, providing a magnificent frame for opposing images. Facing the bleached statue of a police diver is Superintendent James Urquhart of Grampian Police, svelte in a navy jacket and red striped tie, the sober smoothness of his office suit contrasted with the hooded all over rubber suit of the model **[plate 21]**.

More recent history penetrates the present with the still-ongoing investigation of the Lockerbie air crash, which took place on 21 December 1988. Dumfries Police Station has a basement still filled with the accumulated evidence; there is a photo album, labelled *On Eagles' Wings*, which contains the photographs and personal details of everyone who was killed. Brettle's portrait is of the four staffers who have given a large part of their

**18 THE DOW FAMILY**

DETECTIVE CONSTABLE
ANITA DOW
LOTHIAN AND BORDERS POLICE

I am a detective constable in Lothian and Borders Police, currently seconded to the Amethyst Team. I am thirty-seven years old and have ten years police service. I am married to Stuart who is also a police officer. The Amethyst Team is dedicated to taking reports of, and investigating, all sexual assaults on adults and sexual and physical assaults on children within the Edinburgh area. My daily role involves obtaining detailed statements from both adult and child victims, this can, on occasion, take several days or weeks depending on the nature of the abuse being reported and the level of distress suffered by the victim. An important part of my role when dealing with victims is to gain their trust, allowing them to feel comfortable talking in detail about what has happened to them. I very much enjoy my current role which is demanding and on occasions can be distressing. It does help that my husband is a police officer and understands the nature of what I am dealing with at work.

PC STUART DOW
ROADS POLICING BRANCH
LOTHIAN AND BORDERS POLICE

I am a constable in Lothian and Borders Police, currently seconded to the Roads Policing Branch. I am married to Anita, who is also a police officer. I am one of nine officers who cover Edinburgh city centre and the surrounding suburbs. My main role is to prevent and reduce road accidents. This is achieved by education and enforcement. My day-to-day duties involve attending the scene of crashes, ranging from minor collisions to serious incidents. Where there are fatalities I am responsible for reporting the facts to the Procurator Fiscal and carrying out enquiries on their behalf. I have been trained as a family liaison officer, which means I am deployed as the single point of contact between a victim's family and the enquiry team in serious and fatal road traffic collisions. I have to keep the victim's family informed of the circumstances and make sure they understand the legal protocols involved.

**19 FIREARMS SUPPORT UNIT**
LOTHIAN AND BORDERS POLICE

The Firearms Support Unit has five specialised support functions and is responsible for attending all incidents involving the criminal use of firearms in the Lothian and Borders area. The Tactical Firearms Unit has in excess of 100 firearms officers who are based at territorial divisions and are called out when required. The Armed Response Vehicle Unit has two armed response vehicles that are manned around the clock. The Airport Security Unit provides armed cover at Edinburgh Airport. The Security and Protection Unit provides close protection to VIPs. The Operational Training Unit consists of qualified instructors who provide all firearms training and are also operational firearms officers in their own right. Each instructor has an area of expertise such as close protection or rifle and all are qualified firearms tactics advisers. Instructors take turns on-call to give advice to commanders dealing with armed incidents.

**20 PC ALAN MURRAY**
DOG HANDLER
LOTHIAN AND BORDERS POLICE

I am an instructor with responsibility for training dogs and their handlers in specialist roles such as explosives, drugs, weapons, money and tactical firearms. At the end of my day, like all police dog handlers, I take my work home with me. This job is a huge commitment and involves your whole family. It's my job to train puppies for other handlers; a puppy will come to me when it's about eight weeks old and won't leave my house for the first five months of its life. Then it joins the rest of the dogs in purpose-built kennels in my back garden. It is at this early stage of the dog's life that my wife and three children play an important part in the socialisation and training of the pup. Puppies remain with me for up to a year before being allocated to their permanent handlers. I have responsibility for all of these dogs all year round.

**21 SUPERINTENDENT JAMES URQUHART**
HEAD OF OPERATIONAL PLANNING
GRAMPIAN POLICE

The Operational Planning Department is dedicated to security and emergency response. This involves Royalty and VIP security, oil industry liaison, counter terrorism, emergency planning and events co-ordination. The Royalty and VIP Security Unit is responsible for all Royal and VIP visits to the Grampian area. Deeside is home to Balmoral and Birkhall and in 2006 members of the Royal Family spent a total of 220 days in the area. The Oil Industry Liaison Unit is the only police unit of its kind in the UK. The unit has responsibility for policing all offshore installations in UK Scottish waters. Force Counter-Terrorist Security Advisers are responsible for the local delivery of the Protect strand of the UK Government's counter-terrorist strategy. They are also responsible for the security of the Critical National Infrastructure (CNI) sites within the Grampian Police area. Due to the unique role carried out by his department, Superintendent Urquhart is involved in emergency planning policy development across the UK.

professional life to the case: one, Rolf Buwert, is a fluent German speaker whose skills have been called on repeatedly in the long course of the enquiry, and who is retiring with no final conclusion to his life's work. At Brettle's suggestion, they have been photographed beneath the commemorative plaque in the Chapel of Remembrance at Tundergarth, where they take up positions as if attending an unending funeral [plate 22].

The twenty-six exhibits fill an important space in the Scottish National Portrait Gallery's display. We have come a long way since the lone heroism of nineteenth-century solo-portraiture was in fashion. The Portrait Gallery has blazed something of a trail in creating a more collective view of the major public and private sector employers of the region, with Iain Stewart's work on the National Health Service, 1999, and Fionna Carlisle's portraits of the oil industry, 2006. The Gallery policy has been to steer the collection in a different direction, away from the great and the good, if you like, and towards the Common Man. 'And woman', my mind immediately adds, in Jane Brettle's voice, as the image of Deputy Chief Constable Norma Graham arises unbidden to the surface. It was Norma Graham who, Brettle observed, said 'we' rather than 'I' throughout her sitting. Since she described her role as 'building bridges with different communities' this was clearly in character. The hat stand, featured in the background, shows rank with its decorative silver braid; the controlled nerves of its owner are revealed in the hands clasped on the desk before her [plate 23].

This is an inclusive exhibition, inclusive in several senses. It covers the unexpectedly wide scope of police work across an unevenly enormous geographical area, including contour features above and below ground. It notes the social change at work both within the Police Force and the wider community – without ever omitting the ultimately decisive role of the use of force itself. Finally, and typically of the whole trajectory of Brettle's work, it crosses the divide between portraiture and documentary by combining the most lucid and

**22** LOCKERBIE AIR DISASTER
INVESTIGATION OFfiCERS
DUMFRIES AND GALLOWAY
CONSTABULARY

On 21 December 1988 Libyan terrorists blew up Pan Am Flight 103. Major parts of the debris landed in Lockerbie. Tom Gordon was the senior investigating officer at Lockerbie prior to his retirement. He now holds a civilian post at police headquarters and is still involved in the Lockerbie case in an advisory capacity. Detective Constable Karen Rice was involved in the difficult task of identifying and returning victims' personal effects. She developed close links with the victims' families and was highly regarded by many of them. In recognition of her work she was awarded the British Empire Medal. Constable Rolf Buwert is the community constable at Thornhill, a small rural station. Rolf was a traffic patrol officer in Lockerbie at the time of the bombing. He is a fluent German speaker, a skill that has been called upon frequently throughout the eight years he spent on the investigation, with Germany and Switzerland being the focus of many enquiries. Detective Chief Inspector Michael Dalgleish is the current senior investigating officer for the Lockerbie Disaster. When the plane struck Lockerbie he was a very young constable and was involved in harrowing mortuary duties, dealing with the remains of the 270 deceased.

**23** DEPUTY CHIEF
CONSTABLE
NORMA GRAHAM
FIFE CONSTABULARY

Having joined the police service in 1981, I served in a number of uniform and detective roles in Edinburgh and the Lothians, including head of the force drug squad and crime management, and later as lead staff officer for HM Inspectorate of Constabulary for Scotland. I was appointed to my current role with Fife Constabulary in November 2005 and, currently, I am the highest-ranking woman police officer in Scotland. My primary role is to work with the police authority and the chief constable to set the strategic direction of policing in Fife with specific responsibility for performance, strategic development, professional standards, human resources, finance and criminal justice.

acute images of individuals with all the necessary visual clues to describe a working lifestyle. In so doing it also achieves the unexpected: a photographer whose meticulous artistry is inimical to the very concept of 'snapshot photography' has provided her audience with a vivid slice-of-life take on where the force has integrated itself into the society it has a remit to control.

*Amanda Hopkinson is Director of the British Centre for Literary Translation, School of Literature and Creative Writing, University of East Anglia.*

1. Author of the endnotes to *airside*, City Art Centre, Edinburgh, 2003.

2. See the introduction, p. 12, to Amanda Hopkinson, *Julia Margaret Cameron*, Virago, 1988.

3. Personal letter from Jane Brettle, dated 9 October 2006.

4. Jane Brettle has worked extensively with siteworks and public art installations across Scotland, as well as with the Fitzwilliam Museum, Cambridge and Cambridge University Department of Architecture, 1995 and the Henry Moore Institute, Leeds, 1998.

**24 STRANRAER PORTS OFFICERS**
DUMFRIES AND GALLOWAY CONSTABULARY

Dumfries and Galloway Constabulary Ports Unit police the ports of Stranraer and Cairnryan, which provide the ferry services from mainland UK to Northern Ireland. There are around thirty sailings a day from the ports with nearly two million passengers and 800,000 vehicles using these services in 2005. There are forty-five police officers and twenty-seven civilian support staff deployed in various roles within the unit. Staff are expected to deal with anything from a missing person to a lorry load of contraband cigarettes or people being smuggled into the UK. They work closely with the carriers, HM Revenue and Customs, the UK Immigration Service and the Department for Work and Pensions. One of the most significant changes in the work of the ports unit over the last few years has been in the increased number of failed asylum seekers and illegal immigrants traced at the ports. In 2005 a total of sixty-seven different nationalities were traced travelling through the ports and a significant number arrested. The Small Ports Policing Team also patrols the region's coastline and the ninety-one small ports scattered across the area.

# FORCE: A CONTEMPORARY PORTRAIT OF SCOTLAND'S POLICE
## PHOTOGRAPHS BY JANE BRETTLE

**Front cover  PC John Bryden**
Wildlife Crime Officer, Northern Constabulary
Lochailort, West Highlands 2006

**1  Air Support Unit**
Strathclyde Police
PC Kevin Brown
Sergeant John Watt
PC Nicholas Whyte
PC Joseph Moore
PC Graham Watson
PC Jerome Callan
Inspector David Dick
The Heliport, Glasgow 2006

**2  Detective Sergeant David Nolan**
Computer Crime Unit, Central Scotland Police
Falkirk Police Station 2006

**3  Community Support Unit**
Lothian and Borders Police, O Division
**Sergeant Gary Russell** Police Search Adviser (POLSA), PSU, Marine Unit
**PC Craig Carse** PSU, CBRN, Search
**PC Brian Suddon** PSU, CBRN, Search, Marine Unit
**PC Darren Cook** PSU, CBRN, Search
**PC Lorna Scott** PSU, CBRN, Search
**Chief Superintendent Fiona Taylor**
Public Order Commander
Bangour Village Hospital, West Lothian 2006

**4  Special PC Trevor Killen**
Radio Operations, RAF Kinloss, Grampian Constabulary
**Sergeant Gavin Thornton,** Air Traffic Control
**Flight Lieutenant Justin Owen** Nimrod Pilot
RAF Kinloss, Aberdeenshire 2006

**5 National Support Staff**
Lothian and Borders Police
**Inspector David Lyle** Scottish Co-ordinator, the Gay Police Association
**Inspector Dinesh Joshi MBE** Supporting Ethnic Minority Police Staff for Equality in Race (SEMPERscotland)
**Tricia Cochrane** Committee member British Association of Women in Policing (BAWP), Women's Development Forum (WDF) Scotland Lothian and Borders Police Headquarters, Edinburgh 2006

**6 PC Wendy Blair**
Asylum Liaison Unit, Strathclyde Police, E Division
with **Dilshad Ahmad** Interpreter
Shervin Nayery
Zerdi Suren
Hanim Suren
**Dayna Carcary** Interpreter
Tron St Mary's Church, Glasgow 2006

**7 Police Forensic Science Laboratory**
Tayside Police
**Steve McCartney** Advanced Reporting Scientist, Chemistry Section
**Derek Bain** Head of Chemistry Section
**Elizabeth Bain** Advanced Reporting Forensic Scientist, Biology Section
**Ben Mallinder** Advanced Reporting Forensic Scientist, Biology Section
Biology Laboratory, Tayside Police Headquarters, Dundee 2006
Police Forensic Science Laboratory, Tayside Police
**Alastair Burt** Team Leader, Biology Section
**Sarah Pheasey** Advanced Reporting Forensic Scientist, Biology Section
**Fariha Abidi** Advanced Reporting Forensic Scientist, Biology Section
**Gwen Teppett** Senior Forensic Scientist, Biology Section
Scene of Crime, Rankin House, University of Abertay, Dundee 2006

Police Forensic Science Laboratory, Tayside Police
**Yvonne McLaren** Team Leader, Biology Section
**Kathy Robertson** Senior Forensic Scientist, DNA, Biology Section
**Mike Baxter** Head of Police Forensic Science Laboratory
Sheriff Court, Dundee 2006
**Debbie Auras** Temporary Assistant Forensic Scientist, Biology Section
**Fiona Murrie** Assistant Forensic Scientist, Biology Section
**Tom Ross** DNA database Office Manager/Liaison Officer
DNA Database Analysis Office, Tayside Police Headquarters, Dundee 2006

**8 Violence Reduction Unit**
Strathclyde Police
**David Koppel** Clinical Director, Consultant Craniofacial/Oral & Maxillofacial Surgeon
Regional Maxillofacial Unit, Southern General Hospital
**Dr Christine Goodall** Clinical Lecturer in Oral Surgery, Glasgow University Dental School
**Karyn McCluskey** Deputy Head, Violence Reduction Unit, Strathclyde Police
Southern General Hospital, Glasgow 2006

**9 PC Keith Mulloy**
School Based Police Officer, Grampian Police
**with Mark Reid, Liam Simpson, Kristopher Reid, David Spence, Jodie Reid, Nicole Scott**
Northfield Academy, Aberdeen 2006

**10 Mounted Section**
Lothian and Borders Police, O Division
**PC Jim Baker and Commander and PC Jackie Jack and Merlin**
Lothian and Borders Police Headquarters, Edinburgh 2006

**11 Acting Sergeant Philip Johnstone and PC Neil Graham**
Community Police Officers, Dumfries and Galloway Constabulary
Powfoot, Annan 2006

**12 PC Scott Haig**
Northern Constabulary
**with Janette, Lucy and Ross Haig**
The Police House, Baltasound, Unst, Shetland 2006

**13 Inspector Ian Reid**
Royalty and VIP Planning Unit, Grampian Police
**with Major Alex Hutton Her Majesty The Queen's Guard Commander**
Victoria Barracks, Ballater, Aberdeenshire 2006

**14 Football Match Commands**
Strathclyde Police, E Division
**Superintendent Alex McAllister:** Ground Commander
**Sergeant Karen Dickson**
**Ms Isobel Barr**
**Inspector Craig Walker**
**PC Gillian Crofts**
**PC Iain Gibb**
Strathclyde Police, G Division
**Chief Superintendent Robin Howe** Match Commander
**PC Peter Kavanagh**
**Sergeant Alan Wright**
**PC Linsey Stewart**
**Sergeant Craig Smith**
**Inspector Drew Innes**
Hampden Stadium, Glasgow 2006

**15 PC Jeff Adams**
Diving Supervisor, Underwater Search Unit, Central Scotland Police
**with pupils from Trossachs and Lochearnhead Primary Schools**
Loch Venachar, Perthshire 2006

**16 Detective Constable Neill Bingham**
Criminal Justice Department, Fife Constabulary
Video Identification Parade Suite, Kirkcaldy Police Station, Fife 2006

**17 Inspector Graham Gibb MBE**
Operational Support Division, Grampian Police
The Mountain Rescue Centre, Braemar, Aberdeenshire 2006

**18 The Dow Family**
**Detective Constable Anita Dow**
Amethyst Team, Lothian and Borders Police
**PC Stuart Dow** Roads Policing Branch, Lothian and Borders Police
**with Lewis Dow**
The Family Unit, Lothian and Borders Police Headquarters, Edinburgh 2006

**19 Firearms Support Unit**
Lothian and Borders Police, O Division
**Inspector Cameron Chapman** Rifle Officer
**Detective Sergeant Keith Millar** Close Protection Officer
**PC Keith Mailer** ARV Officer
**PC David Reynolds** ARV Officer
**PC Mark McDonald** Airport Officer
**PC Louis Claes** Camouflage Rifle Officer
St Margaret's House, Edinburgh 2006

**20 PC Alan Murray**
Dog Handler, Lothian and Borders Police
**with Ross, Angie, Corrie, and Lyle Murray and Sol**
Edinburgh 2006

**21 Superintendent James Urquhart**
Head of Operational Planning, Grampian Police
The Maritime Museum, Aberdeen 2006

# JANE BRETTLE

**22 Lockerbie Air Disaster Investigation Officers**
Dumfries and Galloway Constabulary
**Detective Chief Inspector Michael Dalgleish** Crime Management Services
**Detective Constable Karen Rice** Family Protection Unit
**PC Rolf Buwert** Community Constable
**Tom Gordon** Executive Support Manager
The Chapel of Rememberance, Tundergarth, Dumfries and Galloway, 2006

**23 Deputy Chief Constable Norma Graham**
Fife Constabulary
Police Headquarters Glenrothes, Fife 2006

**24 Stranraer Ports Officers**
Dumfries and Galloway Constabulary
**PC Kirsty Harrison** Ports Officer
**Tom Buchanan** CCTV Administrator
**SO Alec Whannel and Max** Ports Support Officer
**Detective Constable Gary Ferguson** Ports Officer
**Rob Tossnie** HMRC Officer
**Sergeant Colin Shankly** UKIS Police Command Team
Stranraer Port Police Station, Stranraer, Galloway 2006

**Back cover  Police Training**
Probationer Training Class
Attempted Fraud
**PC Ritchie Macrae** Strathclyde Police
**PC Jan Scott** Strathclyde Police
**PC Jennifer Fraser** Lothian and Borders Police
Crime Management Division
Detective Training
**Detective Sergeant Stuart Murdoch** Strathclyde Police
**Detective Sergeant Douglas Falconer** Strathclyde Police, seconded to the Scottish Police College
Probationer Training Class
Offensive Weapons Scenario
**PC Fiona Kane** Strathclyde Police
**Don Bowman** Training Staff
**PC Matthew Spencer** Fife Constabulary
The Scottish Police College, Tulliallan, Kincardine, Fife 2006

Jane Brettle is an artist based in Edinburgh. She was born in Bristol and has lived in Scotland since 1973. She is also an Associate Senior Lecturer in Contemporary Photographic Practice at the University of Northumbria. She studied Fine Art and Photography in Bristol, Sunderland and Derby.

Her work has been exhibited and published both nationally and internationally, most recently in 2006 at the Kunsthalle Palazzo, Liestal, Switzerland and the Scottish National Portrait Gallery in Edinburgh. She previously established photography projects and facilities in Scotland including Photography Workshop and Portfolio Gallery in Edinburgh. She was a founding director of Fotofeis (the Scottish International Festival of Photography). Brettle's work is in the following collections: the Deutsche Bank Collection, Glasgow Museums and Art Galleries, the Scottish Arts Council, Edinburgh, the City Art Centre, Edinburgh, The MAG Collection Ferens Art Gallery, Hull, the National Galleries of Scotland and also in private national and international collections.

Published by the Trustees of the National Galleries of Scotland for the exhibition *Force: A Contemporary Portrait of Scotland's Police* held at the Scottish National Portrait Gallery, Edinburgh from 4 May to 15 June 2007.

Photographs © Jane Brettle
Text © Louise Jackson and the Trustees of the National Galleries of Scotland, 2007
Text © Amanda Hopkinson and the Trustees of the National Galleries of Scotland, 2007

ISBN 978 1 903278 81 9

Designed and typeset in Gill Sans by Dalrymple
Printed by Cambridge University Press

Front cover: PC John Bryden
Back cover: The Scottish Police College

Scottish Executive
New Arts Sponsorship Awards
In conjunction with